# DIARY OF A
# GOD-MAN
# CHILDREN'S LITURGY

## created by kids for kids

## advent, christmas &
## winter ordinary time
## YEAR C

TREATY OAK PUBLISHERS

# PUBLISHER'S NOTE

DIARY OF A GOD-MAN, all versions, is a work of personal inspiration, providing text and illustrations for children in a series covering the liturgical year.

Excerpts from the *Lectionary for Mass for Use in the Dioceses of the United States of America, second typical edition* © 2001, 1998, 1997, 1986, 1970 Confraternity of Christian Doctrine, Inc., Washington, D.C. Used with permission. All rights reserved. No portion of this text may be reproduced by any means without permission in writing from the copyright owner.

Link to website and other info:
www.diaryofagodman.com
godman82020@gmail.com
@diary_of_a_godman - Instagram
@DiaryofaGodMan - Facebook

Published and printed in the United States of America

## TREATY OAK PUBLISHERS

ISBN - 978-1-943658-87-9

Available in print and digital from Amazon

# DEDICATION

This book is dedicated to our Heavenly Mother, the Blessed, Ever-Virgin, Mary, the Mother of God.

"The One Who is the wisdom of the Father, put His arms around her neck, the One Who is the strength, that gives movement to everything sat in her arms. He Who is the rest of souls, (Mt 11:29) rested on her motherly breast. How gently He held her in His hands, peacefully looked at her, He Whom the angels wish to contemplate (1 Pet 1:12) and He gently called her, He Whom every being calls upon when in need. Filled with the Holy Spirit, she held Him close to her heart … She never had enough of seeing Him or of hearing Him, Whom "many prophets and kings wished to see … but did not see." (Lk 10:24) Thus Mary grew evermore in love and her mind was unceasingly attached to divine contemplation."

– St Amadeus of Lausanne (1108-1159) Bishop
(Homily on the Motherhood of Mary, 4).

# TABLE OF CONTENTS

## advent, christmas &
## winter ordinary time
## YEAR C

# DIARY OF A GOD-MAN CHARACTERS

God the Father      God the Son      God the Holy Spirit

Aaron    Sons of Aaron    Abishai    Abner

Adam    Andrew    Annas    Caesar Augustus

Bartholomew    Caiaphas    David    Elijah

Elizabeth    Eve    Ezra    Gabriel

Herod    Isaiah    James    James the Lesser

Jeremiah

John

John the Baptist

Joseph

Judas

Luke

Lysanias

Magi

Mary

Mary Magdalen

Matthew

Micah

Moses

Paul

Peter

Philip

Philip Tetrarch

Pontius Pilot

Saul

Simon

Thadius

Thomas

Tiberius Caesar

Titus

# CAN YOU FIND THESE GENEROUS SUPPORTERS IN THE BOOK?

 Kevin Dickinson

 Tiffany Dickinson

 Gabbi Dickinson

 Grace Dickinson

 Joseph Dickinson

 Ann Marie Dickinson

 Elijah Dickinson

 Catherine Dickinson

 Andrew Adams

 Ronnie Adams

 Marci Adams

 Wes Adams

 Greg Arend

 Lacey Arend

 Linda Arend

 Coach TJ Barnes

 Kate Blew

 Jameson Brannon

 Fr. John Connell

David Gudorf

Sara Gudorf

Emily Gudorf

Julia Gudorf

Laura Gudorf

Owen Gudorf

Chase Martin

Fletcher Martin

Travis McAfee

Bree McAfee

Jamie McAfee

Caden Medeiros

Abbey Rojeski

Sarah Beth Sammons

Fr. Jason Sharbaugh

Fr. Alex Smith

Dr. Adriana Stacey

Dr. Heath Stacey

Annalise Stacey

Jack Stacey

Mary Virginia Stacey

Whit Stacey

Fr. Jason Tyler

Dr. Darrin Storms

# advent, christmas & winter ordinary time

## YEAR C

# 1ST READING JER 33:14-16

# FIRST SUNDAY OF ADVENT

The days are coming, says the LORD,
when I will fulfill the promise
I made to the house of Israel and Judah.
In those days, in that time,
I will raise up for David a just shoot ;
he shall do what is right and just in the land.
In those days Judah shall be safe
and Jerusalem shall dwell secure;
this is what they shall call her:
"The LORD our justice."

# PS 25:4-5, 8-9, 10, 14

# PSALM TO YOU, O LORD, I LIFT MY SOUL.

Your ways, O LORD, make known to me;
  teach me your paths,
Guide me in your truth and teach me,
  for you are God my savior,
  and for you I wait all the day.

Good and upright is the LORD;
  thus he shows sinners the way.
He guides the humble to justice,
  and teaches the humble his way.

All the paths of the LORD are kindness and constancy
  toward those who keep his covenant and his decrees.
The friendship of the LORD is with those who fear him,
  and his covenant, for their instruction.

Brothers and sisters:
May the Lord make you increase and abound in love
for one another and for all,
just as we have for you,
so as to strengthen your hearts,
to be blameless in holiness before our God and Father
at the coming of our Lord Jesus with all his holy ones.  Amen.

2ND READING
1 Thes 3:12—4:2

Finally, brothers and sisters,
we earnestly ask and exhort you in the Lord Jesus that,
as you received from us
how you should conduct yourselves to please God
and as you are conducting yourselves
you do so even more.
For you know what instructions we gave you through the Lord Jesus.

# GOSPEL Lk 21:25-28, 34-36

Jesus said to his disciples:
"There will be signs in the sun, the moon, and the stars, and on earth nations will be in dismay, perplexed by the roaring of the sea and the waves. People will die of fright in anticipation of what is coming upon the world, for the powers of the heavens will be shaken. And then they will see the Son of Man coming in a cloud with power and great glory. But when these signs begin to happen, stand erect and raise your heads because your redemption is at hand.

"Beware that your hearts do not become drowsy from carousing and drunkenness and the anxieties of daily life, and that day catch you by surprise like a trap. For that day will assault everyone who lives on the face of the earth. Be vigilant at all times and pray that you have the strength to escape the tribulations that are imminent and to stand before the Son of Man."

Jerusalem, take off your robe of mourning and misery;
  put on the splendor of glory from God forever:
wrapped in the cloak of justice from God,
    bear on your head the mitre
    that displays the glory of the eternal name.
For God will show all the earth your splendor:
    you will be named by God forever
    the peace of justice, the glory of God's worship.

**SECOND SUNDAY OF ADVENT**

# 1ST READING BAR 5:1-9

Up, Jerusalem! stand upon the heights;
  look to the east and see your children
gathered from the east and the west
    at the word of the Holy One,
    rejoicing that they are remembered by God.
Led away on foot by their enemies they left you:
    but God will bring them back to you
    borne aloft in glory as on royal thrones.
For God has commanded
    that every lofty mountain be made low,
and that the age–old depths and gorges
    be filled to level ground,
    that Israel may advance secure in the glory of God.
The forests and every fragrant kind of tree
    have overshadowed Israel at God's command;
for God is leading Israel in joy
    by the light of his glory,
    with his mercy and justice for company.

# PSALM

## 126:1-2, 2-3, 4-5, 6

When the LORD brought back the captives
of Zion, we were like men dreaming.
Then our mouth was filled with laughter,
and our tongue with rejoicing.

hen they said among the nations,
"The LORD has done great things for them."
he LORD has done great things for us;
we are glad indeed.

# THE LORD HAS DONE GREAT THINGS FOR US; WE ARE FILLED WITH JOY.

Restore our fortunes, O LORD,
like the torrents in the southern desert.
Those that sow in tears
shall reap rejoicing.

Although they go forth weeping,
carrying the seed to be sown,
They shall come back rejoicing,
carrying their sheaves.

# 2ND READING

## PHIL 1:4-6, 8-11

Brothers and sisters:

I pray always with joy in my every prayer for all of you, because of your partnership for the gospel from the first day until now. I am confident of this, that the one who began a good work in you will continue to complete it until the day of Christ Jesus. God is my witness, how I long for all of you with the affection of Christ Jesus. And this is my prayer: that your love may increase ever more and more in knowledge and every kind of perception, to discern what is of value, so that you may be pure and blameless for the day of Christ, filled with the fruit of righteousness that comes through Jesus Christ for the glory and praise of God.

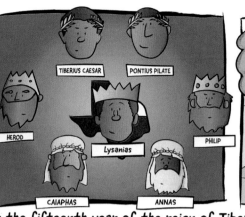

the fifteenth year of the reign of Tiberius Caesar,
when Pontius Pilate was governor of Judea,
and Herod was tetrarch of Galilee,
and his brother Philip tetrarch of the region
of Ituraea and Trachonitis,
and Lysanias was tetrarch of Abilene,
during the high priesthood of Annas and Caiaphas,
the word of God came to John the son of Zechariah in the desert.
John went throughout the whole region of the Jordan,
proclaiming a baptism of repentance for the forgiveness of sins,
as it is written in the book of the words of the prophet Isaiah:

> A voice of one crying out in the desert:
> "Prepare the way of the Lord,
>   make straight his paths.
> Every valley shall be filled
>   and every mountain and hill shall be made low.
> The winding roads shall be made straight,
>   and the rough ways made smooth,
> and all flesh shall see the salvation of God."

GOSPEL

LK 3:1-6

After the man, Adam, had eaten of the tree, the LORD God called to the man and asked him, "Where are you?" He answered, "I heard you in the garden; but I was afraid, because I was naked, so I hid myself."

Then he asked, "Who told you that you were naked? You have eaten, then, from the tree of which I had forbidden you to eat!" The man replied, "The woman whom you put here with me she gave me fruit from the tree, and so I ate it. The LORD God then asked the woman, "Why did you do such a thing?" The woman answered, "The serpent tricked me into it, so I ate it."

Then the LORD God said to the serpent: "Because you have done this, you shall be banned from all the animals and from all the wild creatures; on your belly shall you crawl, and dirt shall you eat all the days of your life. I will put enmity between you and the woman, and between your offspring and hers; he will strike at your head, while you strike at his heel." The man called his wife Eve, because she became the mother of all the living.

# PSALM 98:1, 2-3AB, 3CD-4

Sing to the LORD a new song,
for he has done wondrous deeds;
His right hand has won victory for him,
his holy arm.

The LORD has made his salvation known:
in the sight of the nations he has revealed his justice.
He has remembered his kindness and his faithfulness
toward the house of Israel.

All the ends of the earth have seen
the salvation by our God.
Sing joyfully to the LORD, all you lands;
break into song; sing praise.

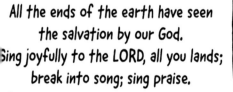

Brothers and sisters: Blessed be the God and Father of our Lord Jesus Christ, who has blessed us in Christ with every spiritual blessing in the heavens, as he chose us in him, before the foundation of the world, to be holy and without blemish before him.

In love he destined us for adoption to himself through Jesus Christ, in accord with the favor of his will, for the praise of the glory of his grace that he granted us in the beloved. In him we were also chosen, destined in accord with the purpose of the One who accomplishes all things according to the intention of his will, so that we might exist for the praise of his glory, we who first hoped in Christ.

The angel Gabriel was sent from God to a town of Galilee called Nazareth, to a virgin betrothed to a man named Joseph, of the house of David, and the virgin's name was Mary. And coming to her, he said, "Hail, full of grace! The Lord is with you." But she was greatly troubled at what was said and pondered what sort of greeting this might be. Then the angel said to her, "Do not be afraid, Mary, for you have found favor with God. Behold, you will conceive in your womb and bear a son, and you shall name him Jesus. He will be great and will be called Son of the Most High, and the Lord God will give him the throne of David his father, and he will rule over the house of Jacob forever, and of his Kingdom there will be no end."

But Mary said to the angel, "How can this be, since I have no relations with a man?" And the angel said to her in reply, "The Holy Spirit will come upon you, and the power of the Most High will overshadow you. Therefore the child to be born will be called holy, the Son of God. And behold, Elizabeth, your relative, has also conceived a son in her old age, and this is the sixth month for her who was called barren; for nothing will be impossible for God." Mary said, "Behold, I am the handmaid of the Lord. May it be done to me according to your word." Then the angel departed from her.

# THIRD SUNDAY OF ADVENT

Shout for joy, O daughter Zion!
　　Sing joyfully, O Israel!
Be glad and exult with all your heart,
　　O daughter Jerusalem!
The LORD has removed the judgment against you
　　he has turned away your enemies;
the King of Israel, the LORD, is in your midst,
　　you have no further misfortune to fear.
On that day, it shall be said to Jerusalem:
　　Fear not, O Zion, be not discouraged!
The LORD, your God, is in your midst,
　　a mighty savior;
he will rejoice over you with gladness,
　　and renew you in his love,
he will sing joyfully because of you,
　　as one sings at festivals.

# 1ST READING
# ZEP 3:14-18A

# PSALM IS 12:2-3, 4, 5-6

## CRY OUT WITH JOY AND GLADNESS: FOR AMONG YOU IS THE GREAT AND HOLY ONE OF ISRAEL.

God indeed is my savior;
    I am confident and unafraid.
My strength and my courage is the LORD,
    and he has been my savior.
With joy you will draw water
    at the fountain of salvation.

Give thanks to the LORD, acclaim his name;
    among the nations make known his deeds,
    proclaim how exalted is his name.

Sing praise to the LORD for his glorious achievement;
    let this be known throughout all the earth.
Shout with exultation, O city of Zion,
    for great in your midst
    is the Holy One of Israel!

Brothers and sisters:
Rejoice in the Lord always.
I shall say it again: rejoice!
Your kindness should be known to all.
The Lord is near.
Have no anxiety at all, but in everything,
by prayer and petition, with thanksgiving,
make your requests known to God.
Then the peace of God that surpasses all understanding
will guard your hearts and minds in Christ Jesus.

## 2ND READING
## PHIL 4:4-7

The crowds asked John the Baptist, "What should we do?" He said to them in reply, "Whoever has two cloaks should share with the person who has none. And whoever has food should do likewise." Even tax collectors came to be baptized and they said to him, "Teacher, what should we do?" He answered them, "Stop collecting more than what is prescribed." Soldiers also asked him, "And what is it that we should do?" He told them, "Do not practice extortion, do not falsely accuse anyone, and be satisfied with your wages."

Now the people were filled with expectation, and all were asking in their hearts whether John might be the Christ. John answered them all, saying, "I am baptizing you with water, but one mightier than I is coming. I am not worthy to loosen the thongs of his sandals. He will baptize you with the Holy Spirit and fire. His winnowing fan is in his hand to clear his threshing floor and to gather the wheat into his barn, but the chaff he will burn with unquenchable fire." Exhorting them in many other ways, he preached good news to the people.

Thus says the LORD:
    You, Bethlehem-Ephrathah
        too small to be among the clans of Judah,
    from you shall come forth for me
        one who is to be ruler in Israel;
    whose origin is from of old,
        from ancient times.
    Therefore the Lord will give them up, until the time
        when she who is to give birth has borne,
    and the rest of his kindred shall return
        to the children of Israel.
    He shall stand firm and shepherd his flock
        by the strength of the LORD,
        in the majestic name of the LORD, his God;
    and they shall remain, for now his greatness
        shall reach to the ends of the earth;
        he shall be peace.

**FOURTH SUNDAY OF ADVENT**

**1ST READING**
**MI 5:1-4A**

Brothers and sisters:
When Christ came into the world, he said:
   "Sacrifice and offering you did not desire,
      but a body you prepared for me;
   in holocausts and sin offerings you took no delight.
   Then I said, 'As is written of me in the scroll,
   behold, I come to do your will, O God.'"

First he says, "Sacrifices and offerings,
holocausts and sin offerings,
you neither desired nor delighted in."
These are offered according to the law.
Then he says, :Behold, I come to do your will."
He takes away the first to establish the second.
By this "will," we have been consecrated
through the offering of the body of Jesus Christ
once for all.

**2ND READING**

**HEB 10:5-10**

# GOSPEL
## Lk 1:39-45

Mary set out
and traveled to the hill country in haste
to a town of Judah,
where she entered the house of Zechariah
and greeted Elizabeth.
When Elizabeth heard Mary's greeting,
the infant leaped in her womb,
and Elizabeth, filled with the Holy Spirit,
cried out in a loud voice and said,
"Blessed are you among women,
and blessed is the fruit of your womb.
And how does this happen to me,
that the mother of my Lord should come to me?
For at the moment the sound of your greeting reached my ears,
the infant in my womb leaped for joy.
Blessed are you who believed
that what was spoken to you by the Lord
would be fulfilled."

The people who walked in darkness
    have seen a great light;
upon those who dwelt in the land of gloom
    a light has shone.
You have brought them abundant joy
    and great rejoicing,
as they rejoice before you as at the harvest,
    as people make merry when dividing spoils.
For the yoke that burdened them,
    the pole on their shoulder,
and the rod of their taskmaster
    you have smashed, as on the day of Midian.
For every boot that tramped in battle,
    every cloak rolled in blood,
    will be burned as fuel for flames.
For a child is born to us, a son is given us;
    upon his shoulder dominion rests.
They name him Wonder-Counselor, God-Hero,
    Father-Forever, Prince of Peace.
His dominion is vast
    and forever peaceful,
from David's throne, and over his kingdom,
    which he confirms and sustains
by judgment and justice,
    both now and forever.
The zeal of the LORD of hosts will do this!

# 96: 1-2, 2-3, 11-12, 13 PSALM

Sing to the LORD a new song;
sing to the LORD, all you lands.
Sing to the LORD; bless his name.

Announce his salvation, day after day.
Tell his glory among the nations;
among all peoples, his wondrous deeds.

## TODAY IS BORN OUR SAVIOR, CHRIST THE LORD.

et the heavens be glad and the earth rejoice;
let the sea and what fills it resound;
let the plains be joyful and all that is in them!
Then shall all the trees of the forest exult.

They shall exult before the LORD, for he comes;
for he comes to rule the earth.
He shall rule the world with justice
and the peoples with his constancy.

# 2ND READING TI 2:11-14

Beloved:
The grace of God has appeared, saving all
and training us to reject godless ways and worldly desires
and to live temperately, justly, and devoutly in this age,
as we await the blessed hope,
the appearance of the glory of our great God
and savior Jesus Christ,
who gave himself for us to deliver us from all lawlessness
and to cleanse for himself a people as his own,
eager to do what is good.

n those days a decree went out from Caesar Augustus that the whole world should be enrolled. This was the first enrollment, when Quirinius was governor of Syria. So all went to be enrolled, each to his own town. And Joseph too went up from Galilee from the town of Nazareth to Judea, to the city of David that is called Bethlehem, because he was of the house and family of David, to be enrolled with Mary, his betrothed, who was with child. While they were there, the time came for her to have her child, and she gave birth to her firstborn son. She wrapped him in swaddling clothes and laid him in a manger, because there was no room for them in the inn.

Now there were shepherds in that region living in the fields and keeping the night watch over their flock. The angel of the Lord appeared to them and the glory of the Lord shone around them, and they were struck with great fear. The angel said to them, "Do not be afraid; for behold, I proclaim to you good news of great joy that will be for all the people. For today in the city of David a savior has been born for you who is Christ and Lord. And this will be a sign for you: you will find an infant wrapped in swaddling clothes and lying in a manger." And suddenly there was a multitude of the heavenly host with the angel, praising God and saying: **LK 2:1-14**

"Glory to God in the highest
and on earth peace to those on whom his favor rests."

# THE HOLY FAMILY OF JESUS MARY AND JOSEPH

# 1ST READING

**SIR 3:2-6, SM 12-14 OR 1:20-22, 24-28**

God sets a father in honor over his children; a mother's authority he confirms over her sons. Whoever honors his father atones for sins, and preserves himself from them. When he prays, he is heard; he stores up riches who reveres his mother. Whoever honors his father is gladdened by children, and, when he prays, is heard. Whoever reveres his father will live a long life; he who obeys his father brings comfort to his mother.

My son, take care of your father when he is old; grieve him not as long as he lives. Even if his mind fail, be considerate of him; revile him not all the days of his life; kindness to a father will not be forgotten, firmly planted against the debt of your sins —a house raised in justice to you.

# PSALM

## 128:1-2, 3, 4-5
### OR 84:2-3, 5-6, 9-10

Blessed is everyone who fears the LORD,
who walks in his ways!
For you shall eat the fruit of your handiwork;
blessed shall you be, and favored.

Your wife shall be like a fruitful vine
in the recesses of your home;
your children like olive plants
around your table.

## BLESSED ARE THOSE WHO FEAR THE LORD AND WALK IN HIS WAYS

Behold, thus is the man blessed
who fears the LORD.
The LORD bless you from Zion:
may you see the prosperity of Jerusalem
all the days of your life.

# 2ND READING COLOSSIANS 3:12-17
### OR 3:12-25 OR 1 JN 3:1-2, 21-24

Brothers and sisters: Put on, as God's chosen ones, holy and beloved, heartfelt compassion, kindness, humility, gentleness, and patience, bearing with one another and forgiving one another, if one has a grievance against another; as the Lord has forgiven you, so must you also do. And over all these put on love, that is, the bond of perfection. And let the peace of Christ control your hearts, the peace into which you were also called in one body.

And be thankful. Let the word of Christ dwell in you richly, as in all wisdom you teach and admonish one another, singing psalms, hymns, and spiritual songs with gratitude in your hearts to God. And whatever you do, in word or in deed, do everything in the name of the Lord Jesus, giving thanks to God the Father through him.

# GOSPEL LK 2:41-52

Each year Jesus' parents went to Jerusalem for the feast of Passover, and when he was twelve years old, they went up according to festival custom. After they had completed its days, as they were returning, the boy Jesus remained behind in Jerusalem, but his parents did not know it. Thinking that he was in the caravan, they journeyed for a day and looked for him among their relatives and acquaintances, but not finding him, they returned to Jerusalem to look for him. After three days they found him in the temple, sitting in the midst of the teachers, listening to them and asking them questions, and all who heard him were astounded at his understanding and his answers. When his parents saw him, they were astonished, and his mother said to him, "Son, why have you done this to us? Your father and I have been looking for you with great anxiety." And he said to them, "Why were you looking for me? Did you not know that I must be in my Father's house?" But they did not understand what he said to them. He went down with them and came to Nazareth, and was obedient to them; and his mother kept all these things in her heart. And Jesus advanced in wisdom and age and favor before God and man.

# 1ST READING NUMBERS 6:22-27

The LORD said to Moses: "Speak to Aaron and his sons and tell them: This is how you shall bless the Israelites. Say to them: The LORD bless you and keep you! The LORD let his face shine upon you, and be gracious to you! The LORD look upon you kindly and give you peace! So shall they invoke my name upon the Israelites, and I will bless them."

# MAY GOD BLESS US IN HIS MERCY

# PSALM 67:2-3, 5, 6, 8

May God have pity on us and bless us;
may he let his face shine upon us.
So may your way be known upon earth;
among all nations, your salvation.

May the nations be glad and exult
because you rule the peoples in equity;
the nations on the earth you guide.

May the peoples praise you, O God;
may all the peoples praise you!
May God bless us,
and may all the ends of the earth fear him!

# 2ND READING GALATIANS 4:4-7

Brothers and sisters: When the fullness of time had come, God sent his Son, born of a woman, born under the law, to ransom those under the law, so that we might receive adoption as sons. As proof that you are sons, God sent the Spirit of his Son into our hearts, crying out, "Abba, Father!" So you are no longer a slave but a son, and if a son then also an heir, through God.

The shepherds went in haste to Bethlehem and found Mary and Joseph, and the infant lying in the manger. When they saw this, they made known the message that had been told them about this child. All who heard it were amazed by what had been told them by the shepherds. And Mary kept all these things, reflecting on them in her heart. Then the shepherds returned, glorifying and praising God for all they had heard and seen, just as it had been told to them.

Then eight days were completed for his circumcision, he was named Jesus, the name given him by the angel before he was conceived in the womb.

Rise up in splendor, Jerusalem! Your light has come, the glory of the Lord shines upon you. See, darkness covers the earth, and thick clouds cover the peoples; but upon you the LORD shines, and over you appears his glory. Nations shall walk by your light, and kings by your shining radiance. Raise your eyes and look about; they all gather and come to you: your sons come from afar, and your daughters in the arms of their nurses.

# THE EPIPHANY OF THE LORD
# 1ST READING ISAIAH 60:1-6

Then you shall be radiant at what you see, your heart shall throb and overflow, for the riches of the sea shall be emptied out before you, the wealth of nations shall be brought to you. Caravans of camels shall fill you, dromedaries from Midian and Ephah; all from Sheba shall come bearing gold and frankincense, and proclaiming the praises of the LORD.

# PSALM 72:1-2, 7-8, 10-11, 12-13

O God, with your judgment endow the king,
and with your justice, the king's son;
He shall govern your people with justice
and your afflicted ones with judgment.

Justice shall flower in his days,
and profound peace, till the moon be no more.
May he rule from sea to sea,
and from the River to the ends of the earth.

## LORD, EVERY NATION ON EARTH WILL ADORE YOU

The kings of Tarshish and the Isles shall offer gifts;
the kings of Arabia and Seba shall bring tribute.
All kings shall pay him homage,
all nations shall serve him.

For he shall rescue the poor when he cries out,
and the afflicted when he has no one to help him.
He shall have pity for the lowly and the poor;
the lives of the poor he shall save.

# 2ND READING EPHESIANS 3:2-3a, 5-6

Brothers and sisters: You have heard of the stewardship of God's grace that was given to me for your benefit, namely, that the mystery was made known to me by revelation. It was not made known to people in other generations as it has now been revealed to his holy apostles and prophets by the Spirit: that the Gentiles are coheirs, members of the same body, and copartners in the promise in Christ Jesus through the gospel.

# GOSPEL MATTHEW 2:1-12

When Jesus was born in Bethlehem of Judea, in the days of King Herod, behold, magi from the east arrived in Jerusalem, saying, "Where is the newborn king of the Jews? We saw his star at its rising and have come to do him homage." When King Herod heard this, he was greatly troubled, and all Jerusalem with him. Assembling all the chief priests and the scribes of the people, He inquired of them where the Christ was to be born. They said to him, "In Bethlehem of Judea, for thus it has been written through the prophet:
And you, Bethlehem, land of Judah,
are by no means least among the rulers of Judah;
since from you shall come a ruler,
who is to shepherd my people Israel."

hen Herod called the magi secretly and ascertained from them the time of the star's appearance. He sent them to Bethlehem and said, "Go and search diligently for the child. When you have found him, ring me word, that I too may go and do him homage. "After their audience with the king they set out. And behold, the star that they had seen at its rising preceded them, until it came and stopped over the place where the child was. They were overjoyed at seeing the star, and on entering the house they saw the child with Mary his mother. They prostrated themselves and did him homage. Then they opened their treasures and offered him gifts of gold, frankincense, and myrrh. And having been warned in a dream not to return to Herod, they departed for their country by another way.

# THE BAPTISM OF THE LORD

# 1ST READING ISAIAH 42:1-4, 6-7

Thus says the LORD: Here is my servant whom I uphold, my chosen one with whom I am pleased, upon whom I have put my spirit; he shall bring forth justice to the nations, not crying out, not shouting, not making his voice heard in the street. A bruised reed he shall not break, and a smoldering wick he shall not quench, until he establishes justice on the earth; the coastlands will wait for his teaching. I, the LORD, have called you for the victory of justice, I have grasped you by the hand; I formed you, and set you as a covenant of the people, a light for the nations, to open the eyes of the blind, to bring out prisoners from confinement, and from the dungeon, those who live in darkness.

# PSALM 29:1-2, 3-4, 3, 9-10

Give to the LORD, you sons of God,
give to the LORD glory and praise,
Give to the LORD the glory due his name;
adore the LORD in holy attire.

## THE LORD WILL BLESS HIS PEOPLE WITH PEACE

The voice of the LORD is over the waters,
the LORD, over vast waters.
The voice of the LORD is mighty;
the voice of the LORD is majestic.

The God of glory thunders,
and in his temple all say, "Glory!"
The LORD is enthroned above the flood;
the LORD is enthroned as king forever.

Peter proceeded to speak to those gathered in the house of Cornelius, saying: "In truth, I see that God shows no partiality. Rather, in every nation whoever fears him and acts uprightly is acceptable to him. You know the word that he sent to the Israelites as he proclaimed peace through Jesus Christ, who is Lord of all, what has happened all over Judea, beginning in Galilee after the baptism that John preached, how God anointed Jesus of Nazareth with the Holy Spirit and power. He went about doing good and healing all those oppressed by the devil, for God was with him."

# GOSPEL Lk 3:15-16, 21-22

The people were filled with expectation, and all were asking in their hearts whether John might be the Christ. John answered them all, saying, "I am baptizing you with water, but one mightier than I is coming. I am not worthy to loosen the thongs of his sandals. He will baptize you with the Holy Spirit and fire."

After all the people had been baptized and Jesus also had been baptized and was praying, heaven was opened and the Holy Spirit descended upon him in bodily form like a dove. And a voice came from heaven, "You are my beloved Son; with you I am well pleased."

# THE SECOND SUNDAY OF ORDINARY TIME
# 1ST READING ISAIAH 62:1-5

For Zion's sake I will not be silent, for Jerusalem's sake I will not be quiet, until her vindication shines forth like the dawn and her victory like a burning torch. Nations shall behold your vindication, and all the kings your glory; you shall be called by a new name pronounced by the mouth of the LORD. You shall be a glorious crown in the hand of the LORD, a royal diadem held by your God.

No more shall people call you "Forsaken," or your land "Desolate," but you shall be called "My Delight," and your land "Espoused." For the LORD delights in you and makes your land his spouse. As a young man marries a virgin, your Builder shall marry you; and as a bridegroom rejoices in his bride so shall your God rejoice in you.

# PSALM 96:1-2, 2-3, 7-8, 9-10

## PROCLAIM HIS MARVELOUS DEEDS TO ALL THE NATIONS.

Sing to the LORD a new song;
  sing to the LORD, all you lands.
Sing to the LORD; bless his name.

Announce his salvation, day after day.
Tell his glory among the nations;
  among all peoples, his wondrous deeds.

Give to the LORD, you families of nations,
  give to the LORD glory and praise;
  give to the LORD the glory due his name!

Worship the LORD in holy attire.
  Tremble before him, all the earth;
Say among the nations: The LORD is king.
  He governs the peoples with equity.

Brothers and sisters:
There are different kinds of spiritual gifts but the same Spirit;
there are different forms of service but the same Lord;
there are different workings but the same God
who produces all of them in everyone.

# 1 Cor 12:4–11

To each individual the manifestation of the Spirit
is given for some benefit.
To one is given through the Spirit the expression of wisdom;
to another, the expression of knowledge according
to another, faith by the same Spirit;
to another, gifts of healing by the one Spirit;
to another, mighty deeds;
to another, prophecy;
to another, discernment of spirits;
to another, varieties of tongues;
to another, interpretation of tongues.
But one and the same Spirit produces all of these,
distributing them individually to each person as he wishes.

There was a wedding at Cana in Galilee, and the mother of Jesus was there. Jesus and his disciples were also invited to the wedding. When the wine ran short, the mother of Jesus said to him, "They have no wine." And Jesus said to her, "Woman, how does your concern affect me? My hour has not yet come." His mother said to the servers, "Do whatever he tells you." Now there were six stone water jars there for Jewish ceremonial washings, each holding twenty to thirty gallons. Jesus told them, "Fill the jars with water." So they filled them to the brim. Then he told them, "Draw some out now and take it to the headwaiter." So they took it. And when the headwaiter tasted the water that had become wine, without knowing where it came from — although the servers who had drawn the water knew —, the headwaiter called the bridegroom and said to him, "Everyone serves good wine first, and then when people have drunk freely, an inferior one; but you have kept the good wine until now." Jesus did this as the beginning of his signs at Cana in Galilee and so revealed his glory, and his disciples began to believe in him.

**GOSPEL**

**Jn 2: 1-11**

Ezra the priest brought the law before the assembly, which consisted of men, women, and those children old enough to understand. Standing at one end of the open place that was before the Water Gate, he read out of the book from daybreak till midday, in the presence of the men, the women, and those children old enough to understand; and all the people listened attentively to the book of the law. Ezra the scribe stood on a wooden platform that had been made for the occasion. He opened the scroll so that all the people might see it — for he was standing higher up than any of the people —; and, as he opened it, all the people rose. Ezra blessed the LORD, the great God, and all the people, their hands raised high, answered, "Amen, amen!" Then they bowed down and prostrated themselves before the LORD, their faces to the ground. Ezra read plainly from the book of the law of God, interpreting it so that all could understand what was read. Then Nehemiah, that is, His Excellency, and Ezra the priest-scribe and the Levites who were instructing the people said to all the people: "Today is holy to the LORD your God. Do not be sad, and do not weep"— for all the people were weeping as they heard the words of the law. He said further: "Go, eat rich foods and drink sweet drinks, and allot portions to those who had nothing prepared; for today is holy to our LORD. Do not be saddened this day, for rejoicing in the LORD must be your strength!"

## 1ST READING
## NEH 8:2-4A, 5-6, 8-10

# 19:8, 9, 10, 15 PSALM

The law of the LORD is perfect,
refreshing the soul;
The decree of the LORD is trustworthy,
giving wisdom to the simple.

The precepts of the LORD are right,
rejoicing the heart;
the command of the LORD is clear,
enlightening the eye.

## YOUR WORDS, LORD, ARE SPIRIT AND LIFE.

The fear of the LORD is pure,
enduring forever;
he ordinances of the LORD are true,
all of them just.

Let the words of my mouth and the thought of my heart
find favor before you,
O LORD, my rock and my redeemer.

# 2ND READING I Cor 12:12–14, 27 or I Cor 12:12–30

Brothers and sisters:
As a body is one though it has many parts,
and all the parts of the body, though many, are one body,
so also Christ.
For in one Spirit we were all baptized into one body,
whether Jews or Greeks, slaves or free persons,
and we were all given to drink of one Spirit.
Now the body is not a single part, but many.
You are Christ's body, and individually parts of it.

Since many have undertaken to compile a narrative of the events
that have been fulfilled among us,
just as those who were eyewitnesses from the beginning
and ministers of the word have handed them down to us,
I too have decided,
after investigating everything accurately anew,
to write it down in an orderly sequence for you,
most excellent Theophilus,
so that you may realize the certainty of the teachings
you have received.

Jesus returned to Galilee in the power of the Spirit,
and news of him spread throughout the whole region.
He taught in their synagogues and was praised by all.

He came to Nazareth, where he had grown up,
and went according to his custom
into the synagogue on the sabbath day.
He stood up to read and was handed a scroll of the prophet Isaiah.
He unrolled the scroll and found the passage where it was written:

> The Spirit of the Lord is upon me,
> because he has anointed me
> to bring glad tidings to the poor.
> He has sent me to proclaim liberty to captives
> and recovery of sight to the blind,
> to let the oppressed go free,
> and to proclaim a year acceptable to the Lord.

Rolling up the scroll, he handed it back to the attendant and sat down,
and the eyes of all in the synagogue looked intently at him.
He said to them,
"Today this Scripture passage is fulfilled in your hearing."

# 4TH SUNDAY IN ORDINARY TIME 1ST READING
## Jer 1:4-5, 17-19

The word of the LORD came to me, saying:

Before I formed you in the womb I knew you,
before you were born I dedicated you,
a prophet to the nations I appointed you.

But do you gird your loins;
stand up and tell them
all that I command you.
Be not crushed on their account,
as though I would leave you crushed before them;
for it is I this day
who have made you a fortified city,
a pillar of iron, a wall of brass,
against the whole land:
against Judah's kings and princes,
against its priests and people.
They will fight against you but not prevail over you,
for I am with you to deliver you, says the LORD.

In you, O LORD, I take refuge;
let me never be put to shame.
In your justice rescue me, and deliver me;
incline your ear to me, and save me.

Be my rock of refuge,
a stronghold to give me safety,
for you are my rock and my fortress.
O my God, rescue me from the hand of the wicked.

# PSALM
## 71:1-2, 3-4, 5-6, 15-17

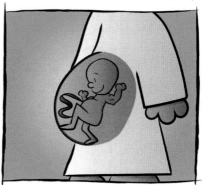

For you are my hope, O Lord;
my trust, O God, from my youth.
On you I depend from birth;
from my mother's womb you are my strength.

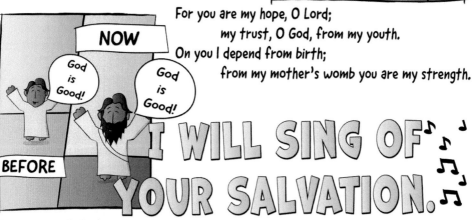

I WILL SING OF YOUR SALVATION.

My mouth shall declare your justice,
day by day your salvation.
O God, you have taught me from my youth,
and till the present I proclaim your wondrous deeds.

Brothers and sisters:
Strive eagerly for the greatest spiritual gifts.
But I shall show you a still more excellent way.

If I speak *in human and angelic tongues,*
but do not have love,
I am a resounding gong or a clashing cymbal.
And if I have the gift of prophecy,
and comprehend all mysteries and all knowledge;
if I have all faith so as to move mountains,
but do not have love, I am nothing.
If I give away everything I own,
and if I hand my body over so that I may boast,
but do not have love, I gain nothing.

Love is patient, love is kind.
It is not jealous, it is not pompous,
It is not inflated, it is not rude,
it does not seek its own interests,
it is not quick-tempered, it does not brood over injury,
it does not rejoice over wrongdoing
but rejoices with the truth.
It bears all things, believes all things,
hopes all things, endures all things.

Love never fails.
If there are prophecies, they will be brought to nothing;
if tongues, they will cease;
if knowledge, it will be brought to nothing.
For we know partially and we prophesy partially,
but when the perfect comes, the partial will pass away.
When I was a child, I used to talk as a child,
think as a child, reason as a child;
when I became a man, I put aside childish things.
At present we see indistinctly, as in a mirror,
but then face to face.
At present I know partially;
then I shall know fully, as I am fully known.
So faith, hope, love remain, these three;
but the greatest of these is love.

Jesus began speaking in the synagogue, saying: "Today this Scripture passage is fulfilled in your hearing." And all spoke highly of him and were amazed at the gracious words that came from his mouth. They also asked, "Isn't this the son of Joseph?" He said to them, "Surely you will quote me this proverb, 'Physician, cure yourself,' and say, 'Do here in your native place the things that we heard were done in Capernaum.'" And he said, "Amen, I say to you, no prophet is accepted in his own native place. Indeed, I tell you, there were many widows in Israel in the days of Elijah when the sky was closed for three and a half

LK 4:21-30

years and a severe famine spread over the entire land. It was to none of these that Elijah was sent, but only to a widow in Zarephath in the land of Sidon. Again, there were many lepers in Israel during the time of Elisha the prophet; yet not one of them was cleansed, but only Naaman the Syrian." When the people in the synagogue heard this, they were all filled with fury. They rose up, drove him out of the town, and led him to the brow of the hill on which their town had been built, to hurl him down headlong. But Jesus passed through the midst of them and went away.

# 5TH SUNDAY IN ORDINARY TIME

In the year King Uzziah died,
I saw the Lord seated on a high and lofty throne,
with the train of his garment filling the temple.
Seraphim were stationed above.

They cried one to the other,
"Holy, holy, holy is the LORD of hosts!
All the earth is filled with his glory!"
At the sound of that cry, the frame of the door shook
and the house was filled with smoke.

## 1ST READING
## IS 6:1-2A, 3-8

Then I said, "Woe is me, I am doomed!
For I am a man of unclean lips,
living among a people of unclean lips;
yet my eyes have seen the King, the LORD of hosts!"
Then one of the seraphim flew to me,
holding an ember that he had taken with tongs from the altar.

He touched my mouth with it, and said,
"See, now that this has touched your lips,
your wickedness is removed, your sin purged."

Then I heard the voice of the Lord saying,
"Whom shall I send? Who will go for us?"
"Here I am," I said; "send me!"

# PSALM
## 138:1-2, 2-3, 4-5, 7-8

I will give thanks to you, O LORD, with all my heart,
for you have heard the words of my mouth;
in the presence of the angels I will sing your praise;
I will worship at your holy temple
and give thanks to your name.

...ecause of your kindness and your truth;
for you have made great above all things
your name and your promise.
...hen I called, you answered me;
you built up strength within me.

...ll the kings of the earth shall give thanks to you, O LORD,
when they hear the words of your mouth;
...nd they shall sing of the ways of the LORD:
"Great is the glory of the LORD."

...our right hand saves me.
The LORD will complete what he has done for me;
...our kindness, O LORD, endures forever;
forsake not the work of your hands.

# IN THE SIGHT OF THE ANGELS
# I WILL SING YOUR PRAISES, LORD.

# 2ND READING 1 COR 15:1-11 OR 1 COR 15:3-8, 11

I am reminding you, brothers and sisters, of the gospel I preached to you, which you indeed received and in which you also stand. Through it you are also being saved, if you hold fast to the word I preached to you, unless you believed in vain. For I handed on to you as of first importance what I also received: that Christ died for our sins in accordance with the Scriptures; that he was buried; that he was raised on the third day in accordance with the Scriptures; that he appeared to Cephas, then to the Twelve. After that, Christ appeared to more than five hundred brothers at once, most of whom are still living, though some have fallen asleep. After that he appeared to James, then to all the apostles. Last of all, as to one born abnormally, he appeared to me. For I am the least of the apostles, not fit to be called an apostle, because I persecuted the church of God. But by the grace of God I am what I am, and his grace to me has not been ineffective. Indeed, I have toiled harder than all of them; not I, however, but the grace of God that is with me. Therefore, whether it be I or they, so we preach and so you believed.

# GOSPEL
## Lk 5:1-11

While the crowd was pressing in on Jesus and listening
to the word of God, he was standing by the Lake of Gennesaret.
He saw two boats there alongside the lake;
the fishermen had disembarked and were washing their nets.
Getting into one of the boats, the one belonging to Simon,
he asked him to put out a short distance from the shore.
Then he sat down and taught the crowds from the boat.
After he had finished speaking, he said to Simon,
"Put out into deep water and lower your nets for a catch."
Simon said in reply,
"Master, we have worked hard all night and have caught nothing,
but at your command I will lower the nets."

When they had done this, they caught a great number of fish
and their nets were tearing.
They signaled to their partners in the other boat
to come to help them.
They came and filled both boats
so that the boats were in danger of sinking.
When Simon Peter saw this, he fell at the knees of Jesus and said,
"Depart from me, Lord, for I am a sinful man."
For astonishment at the catch of fish they had made seized him
and all those with him,
and likewise James and John, the sons of Zebedee,
who were partners of Simon.

Jesus said to Simon, "Do not be afraid;
from now on you will be catching men."
When they brought their boats to the shore,
they left everything and followed him.

# 6TH SUNDAY IN ORDINARY TIME
## 1ST READING JER 17:5-8

Thus says the LORD:

Cursed is the one who trusts in human beings,
who seeks his strength in flesh,
whose heart turns away from the LORD.
He is like a barren bush in the desert
that enjoys no change of season,
but stands in a lava waste,
a salt and empty earth.
Blessed is the one who trusts in the LORD,
whose hope is the LORD.
He is like a tree planted beside the waters
that stretches out its roots to the stream:
it fears not the heat when it comes;
its leaves stay green;
in the year of drought it shows no distress,
but still bears fruit.

# 1:1-2, 3, 4 AND 6 PSALM
## BLESSED ARE THEY WHO HOPE IN THE LORD.

Blessed the man who follows not
the counsel of the wicked,
nor walks in the way of sinners,
nor sits in the company of the insolent,
but delights in the law of the LORD
and meditates on his law day and night.

He is like a tree
planted near running water,
that yields its fruit in due season,
and whose leaves never fade.
Whatever he does, prospers.

Not so the wicked, not so;
they are like chaff which the wind drives away.
For the LORD watches over the way of the just,
but the way of the wicked vanishes.

Brothers and sisters:
If Christ is preached as raised from the dead,
how can some among you say there is no resurrection of the dead?
If the dead are not raised, neither has Christ been raised,
and if Christ has not been raised, your faith is vain;
you are still in your sins.
Then those who have fallen asleep in Christ have perished.
If for this life only we have hoped in Christ,
we are the most pitiable people of all.

# 2ND READING — 1 COR 15:12, 16-20

But now Christ has been raised from the dead,
the firstfruits of those who have fallen asleep.

Jesus came down with the Twelve
and stood on a stretch of level ground
with a great crowd of his disciples
and a large number of the people
from all Judea and Jerusalem
and the coastal region of Tyre and Sidon.
And raising his eyes toward his disciples he said:
    "Blessed are you who are poor,
        for the kingdom of God is yours.
    Blessed are you who are now hungry,
        for you will be satisfied.
    Blessed are you who are now weeping,
        for you will laugh.
    Blessed are you when people hate you,
        and when they exclude and insult you,
        and denounce your name as evil
        on account of the Son of Man.
Rejoice and leap for joy on that day!
Behold, your reward will be great in heaven.
For their ancestors treated the prophets in the same way.
    But woe to you who are rich,
        for you have received your consolation.
    Woe to you who are filled now,
        for you will be hungry.
    Woe to you who laugh now,
        for you will grieve and weep.
    Woe to you when all speak well of you,
        for their ancestors treated the false prophets in this way."

GOSPEL

LK 6, 17. 20-26

# 7TH SUNDAY IN ORDINARY TIME
## 1ST READING  1 SM 26:2, 7-9, 12-13, 22-23

In those days, Saul went down to the desert of Ziph with three thousand picked men of Israel, to search for David in the desert of Ziph. So David and Abishai went among Saul's soldiers by night and found Saul lying asleep within the barricade, with his spear thrust into the ground at his head and Abner and his men sleeping around him.

Abishai whispered to David: "God has delivered your enemy into your grasp this day. Let me nail him to the ground with one thrust of the spear; I will not need a second thrust!" But David said to Abishai, "Do not harm him, for who can lay hands on the LORD's anointed and remain unpunished?" So David took the spear and the water jug from their place at Saul's head, and they got away without anyone's seeing or knowing or awakening. All remained asleep, because the LORD had put them into a deep slumber.

Going across to an opposite slope, David stood on a remote hilltop at a great distance from Abner, son of Ner, and the troops. He said: "Here is the king's spear. Let an attendant come over to get it. The LORD will reward each man for his justice and faithfulness. Today, though the LORD delivered you into my grasp, I would not harm the LORD's anointed."

# 103:1-2, 3-4, 8, 10, 12-13 PSALM

Bless the LORD, O my soul;
    and all my being, bless his holy name.
Bless the LORD, O my soul,
    and forget not all his benefits.

He pardons all your iniquities,
    heals all your ills.
He redeems your life from destruction,
    crowns you with kindness and compassion.

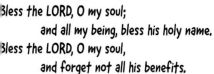

## THE LORD IS KIND AND MERCIFUL.

Merciful and gracious is the LORD,
    slow to anger and abounding in kindness.
Not according to our sins does he deal with us,
    nor does he requite us according to our crimes.

As far as the east is from the west,
    so far has he put our transgressions from us.
As a father has compassion on his children,
    so the LORD has compassion on those who fear him.

# 2ND READING 1 COR 15:45-49

Brothers and sisters:
It is written, *The first man, Adam, became a living being,*
the last Adam a life-giving spirit.
But the spiritual was not first;
rather the natural and then the spiritual.
The first man was from the earth, earthly;
the second man, from heaven.
As was the earthly one, so also are the earthly,
and as is the heavenly one, so also are the heavenly.
Just as we have borne the image of the earthly one,
we shall also bear the image of the heavenly one.

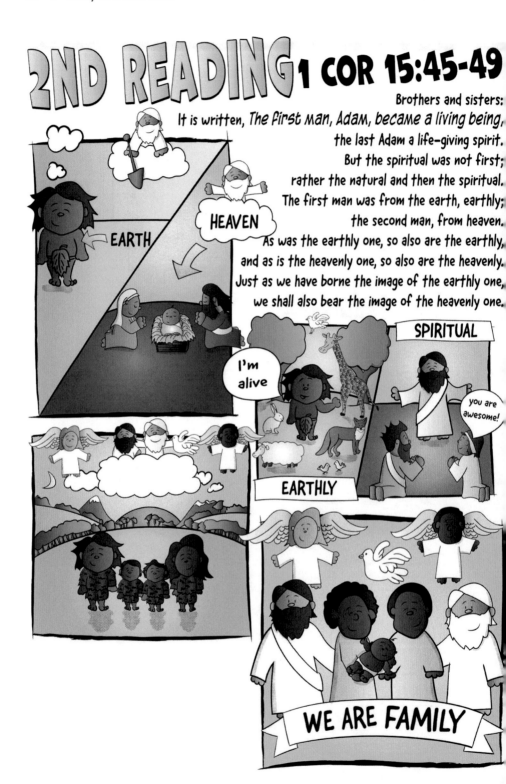

Jesus said to his disciples: "To you who hear I say, love your enemies, do good to those who hate you, bless those who curse you, pray for those who mistreat you. To the person who strikes you on one cheek, offer the other one as well, and from the person who takes your cloak, do not withhold even your tunic. Give to everyone who asks of you, and from the one who takes what is yours do not demand it back. Do to others as you would have them do to you. For if you love those who love you, what credit is that to you? Even sinners love those who love them. And if you do good to those who do good to you, what credit is that to you? Even sinners do the same. If you lend money to those from whom you expect repayment, what credit is that to you? Even sinners lend to sinners, and get back the same amount. But rather, love your enemies and do good to them, and lend expecting nothing back; then your reward will be great

"Stop judging and you will not be judged. Stop condemning and you will not be condemned. Forgive and you will be forgiven. Give, and gifts will be given to you; a good measure, packed together, shaken down, and overflowing, will be poured into your lap. For the measure with which you measure will in return be measured out to you."

# 1ST READING SIR 27:4-7
# 8TH SUNDAY IN ORDINARY TIME

When a sieve is shaken, the husks appear;
so do one's faults when one speaks.
As the test of what the potter molds is in the furnace,
so in tribulation is the test of the just.
The fruit of a tree shows the care it has had;
so too does one's speech disclose the bent of one's mind.
Praise no one before he speaks,
for it is then that people are tested.

# PSALM
## 92:2-3, 13-14, 15-16

It is good to give thanks to the LORD,
to sing praise to your name, Most High,
To proclaim your kindness at dawn
and your faithfulness throughout the night.

# LORD, IT IS GOOD TO GIVE THANKS TO YOU.

The just one shall flourish like the palm tree,
like a cedar of Lebanon shall he grow.
They that are planted in the house of the LORD
shall flourish in the courts of our God.

They shall bear fruit even in old age;
vigorous and sturdy shall they be,
Declaring how just is the LORD,
my rock, in whom there is no wrong.

# 2ND READING
## 1 COR 15:54-58

Brothers and sisters:
When this which is corruptible clothes itself with incorruptibility
and this which is mortal clothes itself with immortality,
then the word that is written shall come about:
*Death is swallowed up in victory.*
*Where, O death, is your victory?*
*Where, O death, is your sting?*
The sting of death is sin,
and the power of sin is the law.
But thanks be to God who gives us the victory
through our Lord Jesus Christ.

Therefore, my beloved brothers and sisters,
be firm, steadfast, always fully devoted to the work of the Lord,
knowing that in the Lord your labor is not in vain.

Jesus told his disciples a parable, "Can a blind person guide a blind person? Will not both fall into a pit? No disciple is superior to the teacher; but when fully trained, every disciple will be like his teacher. Why do you notice the splinter in your brother's eye, but do not perceive the wooden beam in your own? How can you say to your brother, 'Brother, let me remove that splinter in your eye,' when you do not even notice the wooden beam in your own eye? You hypocrite! Remove the wooden beam from your eye first; then you will see clearly to remove the splinter in your brother's eye.

"A good tree does not bear rotten fruit, nor does a rotten tree bear good fruit. For every tree is known by its own fruit. For people do not pick figs from thornbushes, nor do they gather grapes from brambles. A good person out of the store of goodness in his heart produces good, but an evil person out of a store of evil produces evil; for from the fullness of the heart the mouth speaks."

# SPECIAL THANKS TO

All of our Kickstarter Supporters - Without your support, this book series would not have been possible.

Travis McAfee - You are an amazing illustrator and an even better friend. We are truly blessed to have you in our life!

Cynthia Stone - You have gone above and beyond in your guidance in navigating the publishing world. You have provided us the peace of mind that is so valuable for first-time authors.

Monsignor David LeSieur - You have been a great spiritual advisor and have helped rein in some of our wild ideas!

All the priest, leaders, volunteers, and staff at Saint Raphael's in Springdale, Arkansas, and their Children's Liturgy program, which was the launching pad for the concept of the book. - You have all played a large part in helping this concept develop into what it is today.

Veronica Dixon for helping us translate the cartoon bubbles to Spanish.

Startup Junkie - for the initial funding through their business pitch contest.

# created by kids for kids

The Dickinson family—Gabbi, Grace, Joseph, Ann Marie, Elijah, and Catherine, along with their mom, Tiffany—discuss the scriptures and create drawings to tell the stories. Their dad, Kevin, sends them to Travis, who creates the colorful story panels. Monsignor David, our spiritual director, reviews them, and Mom sends adjustments to Travis.

Once everything is finished, we send all our work to Cynthia Stone at Treaty Oak Publishers. She formats the pages to put this book together and oversees the details to publish it.

# ABOUT THE DICKINSON FAMILY

We are a family of 8 who loves our Faith & our Family. When we are not running to and from Sports, Dance and other activities, we love to spend time with each other, our friends and church community.

Tiffany and Kevin Dickinson, parents - Kids' Assistants
Gabrielle, 15, is the Business Manager and handles all finances
Grace, 13, is the Director of Sales
Joseph, 12, is the Head Kids Illustrator
Ann Marie, 10, is the Digital Marketing Manager
Elijah, 8, keeps the energy going
Catherine, 5, Well, she's cute and loves Jesus! She has some pretty interesting ideas!

Made in the USA
Coppell, TX
06 April 2022

76109100R00052